Horseman

by S. Daly Sweeney

Single copies of plays are sold for reading purposes only. The copying or duplicating of a play, or any part of play, by hand or by any other process, is an infringement of the copyright. Such infringement will be vigorously prosecuted.

Baker's Plays
7611 Sunset Blvd.
Los Angeles, CA 90042
bakersplays.com

NOTICE

This book is offered for sale at the price quoted only on the understanding that, if any additional copies of the whole or any part are necessary for its production, such additional copies will be purchased. The attention of all purchasers is directed to the following: this work is fully protected under the copyright laws of the United States of America, the British Commonwealth, including Canada, and all other countries of the Copyright Union. Violations of the Copyright Law are punishable by fine or imprisonment, or both. The copying or duplication of this work or any part of this work, by hand or by any process, is an infringement of the copyright and will be vigorously prosecuted.

This play may not be produced by amateurs or professionals for public or private performance without first submitting application for performing rights. Royalties are due on all performances whether for charity or gain, or whether admission is charged or not. Since performance of this play without the payment of the royalty fee renders anybody participating liable to severe penalties imposed by the law, anybody acting in this play should be sure, before doing so, that the royalty fee has been paid. Professional rights, reading rights, radio broadcasting, television and all mechanical rights, etc. are strictly reserved. Application for performing rights should be made directly to BAKER'S PLAYS.

No one shall commit or authorize any act or omission by which the copyright of, or the right to copyright, this play may be impaired. No one shall make any changes in this play for the purpose of production.

Publication of this play does not imply availability for performance. Both amateurs and professionals considering a production are strongly advised in their own interest to apply to Baker's Plays for written permission before starting rehearsals, advertising, or booking a theatre.

Whenever the play is produced, the author's name must be carried in all publicity, advertising and programs. Also, the following notice must appear on all printed programs, "Produced by special arrangement with Baker's Plays."

Licensing fees for HORSEMAN are based on a per performance rate
and payable one week in advance of the production.

Please consult the Baker's Plays website at www.bakersplays.com or our
current print catalogue for up to date licensing fee information.

Copyright © 2010 by S. Daly Sweeney
Made in U.S.A.
All rights reserved.

HORSEMAN
ISBN **978-0-87440-263-6**
#2045-B

CHARACTERS

4 Women Narrators
1-11 Male or Females, to play other roles

AUTHOR'S NOTE

HORSEMAN was first written and produced as a readers' theatre piece with actors entering and exiting via traditional repose; a second production used more traditional staging, though actors stayed "in the scene" by freezing in a human backdrop to central action, at the ready to join as called.

In either mode, players come in and out of repose (or on- and offstage) as required, with the exception of the four WOMEN, who remain part of the action throughout. Actors can play more than one part, and certain group parts can easily be combined. With character compression, the scene can be played with as few as five actors or as many as fifteen.

Horseman was originally produced in October 1993 and in October 2004 by members of the International Thespian Society of Penncrest High School in Media, PA.

*(The scene opens with **WOMEN** arranged in an off-center frame that surrounds the action of the scene, rocking, knitting. They are storytellers, weaving a memory for the unseen audience, the unwitting newcomer – us. Each woman has a distinct voice, but each operates as part of a poetic whole.)*

FIRST WOMAN. *(looking off)* Near Tarrytown, there lies a village –

SECOND WOMAN. *(eager)* Sleepy Hollow –

FIRST WOMAN. A peaceful valley –

THIRD WOMAN. *(shakes head glumly)* But all who live there –

FOURTH WOMAN. *(eerily)* Seem to walk in sleep and dreams.

FIRST WOMAN. Where even the children –

SECOND WOMAN. Who walk in its woods –

THIRD WOMAN. See visions –

FOURTH WOMAN. Have trances –

FIRST WOMAN. Hear music –

FOURTH WOMAN. And voices –

SECOND WOMAN. Of long dead soldiers –

THIRD WOMAN. And warrior chiefs.

FIRST WOMAN. But of all the spirits who haunt Sleepy Hollow –

SECOND WOMAN. Of all the dead who cannot rest –

FIRST WOMAN. The greatest is that of the Hessian soldier –

THIRD WOMAN. Who rides each night through all of the town –

FOURTH WOMAN. In desperate search of the head that he lost –

SECOND WOMAN. Struck off by a cannon –

THIRD WOMAN. In furious battle –

FIRST WOMAN. Long years ago.

ALL WOMEN. The Headless Horseman of Sleepy Hollow.
FIRST WOMAN. He rides in shadow –
SECOND WOMAN. But greets the dawn –
THIRD WOMAN. Resting in the tranquil churchyard –
FIRST WOMAN. Where lies his gray and crumbling tomb –
THIRD WOMAN. And next to his grave –
SECOND WOMAN. There lies another –
FIRST WOMAN. Marked by a stone that bears the name –
SECOND WOMAN. Ichabod –
FOURTH WOMAN. Ichabod –
FIRST WOMAN. Ichabod Crane.

(ICHABOD enters stage left. He is dressed foppishly, carries a walking stick and a thick book, which he attempts – clumsily – to read as he slowly crossed to centerstage.)

THIRD WOMAN. He was schoolmaster here –
FIRST WOMAN. Long ago.
SECOND WOMAN. I've seen the stone.
THIRD WOMAN. He was a man who looked his name.

(ICHABOD onstage center)

FIRST WOMAN. He was tall –

(ICHABOD bursts with pride.)

THIRD WOMAN. Too tall –

*(ICHABOD tosses a telling glance at the **WOMAN**.)*

SECOND WOMAN. And thin –
THIRD WOMAN. Too thin.
FIRST WOMAN. And pale and weak –
FOURTH WOMAN. With feet like shovels –

(ICHABOD feverishly examines feet.)

THIRD WOMAN. And tiny green eyes.
ICHABOD. They were hazel!
FOURTH WOMAN. And *greedy.*

(ICHABOD resumes stance for cross.)

FIRST WOMAN. He walked home from the schoolhouse as each evening came
And the children would follow and call out his name.

(**BOYS** *approach from stage right and stage left; they circle* **ICHABOD** *and dodge in and out to startle him.*)

They cried –

BOY ONE. Ichabod!

BOY TWO. Ichabod!

BOYS THREE & FOUR. Ichabod Crane!!

BOY FOUR. Afraid of your shadow –

BOY ONE. Too frightened to fight –

BOY THREE. 'less the ghosts and the ghouls –

BOY TWO. that live deep in the woods –

BOY FOUR. try to snatch you away.

BOY TWO. That's for babies –

BOY THREE. And cowards –

BOY ONE. And children –

BOY TWO. Not men.

BOY ONE. Watch out for the wind!

BOY THREE. It'll carry you off!

BOY FOUR. Scarecrow!

BOY TWO. Scarecrow!

(They run off, giggling.)

ICHABOD. *(pursed lips, outraged)* Now! I don't like that! No sir, not one bit!!

ALL BOYS. Ha ha ha ha!

FIRST OLD WOMAN. The older ones lurked in the woods on his path –

(**BOYS** *creep on from corners of stage opposite* **WOMEN**.)

SECOND OLD WOMAN. And they'd watch him approach on his journey home.

FOURTH OLD WOMAN. *Oh,* he was nervous.

THIRD OLD WOMAN. Afraid of his shadow.

FIRST OLD WOMAN. He'd heard our old stories –

SECOND OLD WOMAN. Believed every one.

FOURTH OLD WOMAN. And as evening approached and the daylight waned,
In deep ghostly voices they'd call out his name.
They called –

BOY TWO. Ichabod...

BOY THREE. Ichabod...

BOY ONE. Ichabod Crane!

BOY FOUR. We want you, schoolmaster!

ICHABOD. *(freezes)* Who...Who...Who is that?

BOY ONE. You cannot hide –

BOY TWO. – From our eyes –

BOY FOUR. – Or our voices –

ICHABOD. I can't see your faces!

BOY TWO. We have none –

BOY THREE. We're dead.

BOY TWO. We'll find you...

BOY THREE. We'll catch you...

BOY TWO. We'll eat you...

ICHABOD. Be gone!!!!

BOY THREE. When you're sleeping...

BOY ONE. And dreaming...

BOY TWO. We'll come in the night...

ICHABOD. *(falls to knees, covers eyes, intones)* Spirit, spirit, go away, come again some other day!

BOY FOUR. *(approaching more closely)* We'll go away...

BOY THREE. *IF* you obey us!

ICHABOD. I'll obey!! I'll obey!! Please leave me alone!

BOY ONE. Good, Master Crane –

BOY FOUR. We will give you your task –

BOY THREE. You must follow our orders –

BOY ONE. What you must do is...uh... *(looks to the others, lost)*

BOY THREE. What you must do is... *(looks to **BOY TWO**)*

ICHABOD. Yes? Yes? Anything! Anything!!
BOY TWO. Run to the village –
BOY FOUR. and kiss Mistress Brown! *(others silently hysterical)*
ICHABOD. The minister's wife?
BOY ONE. On the mouth.
BOY THREE. On the mouth.
THIRD WOMAN. And he did.
SECOND WOMAN. Yes, he did.

> (**BOYS** *run together stage righ;,* **ICHABOD** *picks up and dusts off.*)

FIRST WOMAN. But each dawn awoke a braver man.
FOURTH WOMAN. In the schoolhouse he ruled with an iron stick.

> (**BOYS** *march in again, single file, eyes down, line up in front of* **ICHABOD.**)

ICHABOD. Spare the rod and spoil the child! *(brandishes rod)*
BOY ONE. We're –

> (**ICHABOD** *brandishes stick, mimes swing.*)

BOYS. Ow!
BOY ONE. Not –

> *(mimed swing two)*

BOYS. Ow!
BOY ONE. Spoiled!

> *(mimed swing three)*

BOYS. Ow!!!
ICHABOD. And I'll see that you're not.

> *(grand, flourishing wind up for mimed swing four)*

ALL BOYS. OW!!
ICHABOD. You'll thank me some day.

> (**BOYS** *groan and take reposed spots in corners of upstage area.*)

FIRST WOMAN. But sometimes he'd join in a game with the boys –

SECOND WOMAN. And visit their families –

THIRD WOMAN. If their sisters were pretty –

FOURTH WOMAN. And their mothers good cooks.

SECOND WOMAN. But oh! The young ladies!

(**GIRLS** *enter from opposite sides, meet center, perch prettily on lip of stage.*)

THIRD WOMAN. They fell over him.

FOURTH WOMAN. Thought he had culture.

FIRST WOMAN. And learning.

THIRD WOMAN. And taste.

SECOND WOMAN. He *was* from Connecticut.

THIRD WOMAN. Oh, they'd giggle and blush as they called out his name. They sighed –

GIRL ONE. Ichabod!

GIRL TWO. Ichabod!

ALL GIRLS. Ichabod Crane!

ICHABOD. Hello, ladies.

GIRL ONE. Good afternoon

GIRL TWO. It's lovely today.

GIRL THREE. For a walk –

GIRL TWO. By the river.

GIRL ONE. I'll bring you a lunch!

GIRL TWO. And perhaps you might like?

GIRL THREE. If you could?

GIRL TWO. If you would?

GIRL ONE. Take a moment –

GIRL TWO. To tell us –

GIRL ONE. About your adventures.

GIRL THREE. Or read us a *poem*!

GIRL ONE. Or *write* us a poem!

GIRL TWO. Oh, Ichabod…

GIRL ONE. Ichabod…
GIRL THREE. Ichabod…
ICHABOD. *(debonair)* Yes?
GIRL ONE. Tell me of –
GIRL TWO. Tell me of –
GIRL THREE. Tell me of –
ALL GIRLS. – France *(loud group sigh)*.
ICHABOD. *(pause)* France?
GIRL TWO. France.
ICHABOD. *France. (at a loss)* Well…uh…France, huh?
GIRL THREE. Say something!
GIRL TWO. Say something!
GIRL ONE. Say something French!
ICHABOD. Ah. French. Uh…Oui!!
GIRL ONE. *(all burst into girlish giggling)* He's wonderful!
GIRL TWO. Mrs.
GIRL THREE. Ichabod.
GIRL ONE. Crane.
GIRL THREE. *Madame* Crane.
ALL GIRLS. Ooh.
FIRST WOMAN. But Ichabod had eyes for none other than –
ALL WOMEN. Katerina Van Tassel.

    *(**KATERINA** appears stage left, checking nails, twirling her long, blonde hair.)*

GIRL ONE. She's beautiful.
GIRL TWO. And sweet.
GIRL THREE. And smart.
GIRL TWO. And rich.
ICHABOD. *(snaps to attention)* Rich?
GIRL ONE. I hate her!
KATERINA. *(cool, smiling)* Who asked you?
ICHABOD. *(to himself)* Rich?

    *(**GIRLS** and **ICHABOD** freeze in conversation.)*

SECOND WOMAN. But Katerina was courting a young village man –

(**BROM** *enters from audience.*)

THIRD WOMAN. Brom –

FOURTH WOMAN. Brom Van Brunt.

BROM. *(ala Brando, chest thumping and all)* Katerina!!! Katerina!!!

FIRST WOMAN. A big, strong, local man.

THIRD WOMAN. A wonderful horseman.

FOURTH WOMAN. bit rough 'round the edges.

BROM. *(climbs to stage, kneels)* Katerina. Ah luv yoo.

KATERINA. *(still concentrating on grooming)* How much do you love me?

BROM. *(rises, searches for words)* Uh. I luv yoo…A lot. Duh huh.

KATERINA. Oh, Brom! Stop kidding! Really. How much.

BROM. *(already forgotten)* How much wut?

KATERINA. How much do you love me?

BROM. *(pause)* Ah tole yoo. Ah luv yoo.

KATERINA. Hmph. Brom VAN Brunt, you…you… *(stomps her foot and points offstage, directing him away)*

BROM. Wait! Katerina! Katerina! *(He stumbles to left and freezes.)*

SECOND WOMAN. So when Ichabod Crane became her music tutor –

FOURTH WOMAN. Anything for a dollar –

FIRST WOMAN. Katerina knew how to make Brom take her seriously.

(**ICHABOD** *rises from frozen stance;* **KATERINA** *girlishly dashed to his side.*)

THIRD WOMAN. She'd weep and she'd sigh and she'd whisper his name –

KATERINA. Ichabod…Ichabod…Ichabod Crane!

ICHABOD. Nice place your father's got here.

KATERINA. Oh, how I wish that there was someone who could take me away from all this!

ICHABOD. What's wrong with all this?

KATERINA. Well…someone to share it with me, then.

ICHABOD. *(pleased)* Oh.

SECOND WOMAN. She turned his head.

KATERINA. Would you like to take a walk with me Ichabod?

ICHABOD. Sure!

KATERINA. In the woods?

ICHABOD. *(fearful)* The woods?

KATERINA. *(twirling her hair)* Alone?

ICHABOD. Alone! Oh. *(with understanding)* Alone. Sure!

KATERINA. That'll show Brom VAN Brunt.

(**KATERINA** *and* **ICHABOD** *stroll off left.*)

FIRST WOMAN. And it must have.

FOURTH WOMAN. Because he stopped coming to visit.

BROM. *(quick re-entry from freeze)* Ah know when ahm not wuntit. *(stalks off right)*

SECOND WOMAN. Then came the fall festival at Van Tassel's farm.

FIRST WOMAN. The whole town was there –

(**BOYS & GIRLS** *become active from freezes; group and pairs form, lively interaction is indicated.*)

THIRD WOMAN. Except Ichabod.

FOURTH WOMAN. He was late.

(**ICHABOD** *and* **GUNPOWDER** *appear downstage right. Gunpowder's equine nature is indicated solely by physicality of the actor – no props required.*)

FIRST WOMAN. It was his horse.

FOURTH WOMAN. Gunpowder.

(**GUNPOWDER** *waves and smiles at the audience.*)

SECOND WOMAN. Ichabod begged him.

ICHABOD. Please?

GUNPOWDER. *(crosses arms, shakes head)* Nay.

FOURTH WOMAN. And pushed him.

ICHABOD. *(pushing)* Please?

GUNPOWDER. *(pushing back)* Nay.

THIRD WOMAN. And pulled on his mane.

ICHABOD. *(pulls)* Please?!!

GUNPOWDER. *(insulted)* Nay!

FIRST WOMAN. But he wouldn't budge.

*(**MASTER VAN TASSEL** crosses from left.)*

THIRD WOMAN. Until Master VAN Tassel called the schoolmaster's name. He cried –

MASTER VAN TASSEL. Ichabod, Ichabod, Ichabod Crane! You can't treat a horse like that!

BOYS & GIRLS. *(quick reaction and return)* That's a horse?

MASTER VAN TASSEL. Watch Brom Van Brunt and his fine steed, Daredevil. *(indicates offstage left)* He doesn't need to pull that horse.

ICHABOD. *(mimics smacking horse)* Bad horse.

GUNPOWDER. Nay!

MASTER VAN TASSEL. Come, join the party!

*(leads **ICHABOD** to left of center)*

ICHABOD. Sir…uh…where is your daughter?

MASTER VAN TASSEL. Katerina? She's about. Come. Sit with us.

*(**ICHABOD** sits, **VAN TASSEL** melts into larger portrait.)*

THIRD WOMAN. So Ichabod joined our merry group

FOURTH WOMAN. Of husbands and wives –

FIRST WOMAN. Old men –

SECOND WOMAN. and women –

FIRST WOMAN. I was there –

FOURTH WOMAN. And I –

THIRD WOMAN. I was, too.

FIRST WOMAN. We sat and told stories of Sleepy Hollow –

THIRD WOMAN. Of spirits who walk in the woods at night –

SECOND WOMAN. Demons that snatch you and steal your soul –

FIRST WOMAN. And sell it to the Devil as he dances by moonlight –

FOURTH WOMAN. And of Warrior Chiefs who worship their master –

SECOND WOMAN. Deep in the dead of darkest night.

FIRST WOMAN. And of the Headless Horseman of Sleepy Hollow.

ICHABOD. The what?

ALL WOMEN. The Headless Horseman of Sleepy Hollow.

ICHABOD. Oh. No head, huh?

THIRD WOMAN. Nope.

ICHABOD. Nope?

FIRST WOMAN. None.

ICHABOD. None?

SECOND WOMAN. Gone.

ICHABOD. G…G…Gone?

FIRST WOMAN. And we told the tale.

SECOND WOMAN. Ichabod hung on our every word.

THIRD WOMAN. Asked questions –

FOURTH WOMAN. Said prayers –

FIRST WOMAN. Sweat bullets.

FOURTH WOMAN. Until Master Van Tassel called us all together.

MASTER VAN TASSEL. *(entering the action with* **ALL PLAYERS***)* Everyone!!! Everyone!!! I have an announcement to make!

ICHABOD. *(remains seated on lip of stage)* No head at ALL?!!

MASTER VAN TASSEL. My friends, I am pleased to announce to all of you here that my beautiful daughter, Katerina… *(enters from left to join him)*

KATERINA. Oh, Papa.

MASTER VAN TASSEL. Is going to be married.

ALL YOUNG WOMEN. *(shrieking)* Married!

MASTER VAN TASSEL. To none other than the finest young man in our village, Brom Van Brunt *(enters from right to join him)*

YOUNG PEOPLE. Brom Van Brunt!

BROM. *(taking* **KATERINA***'s hands, joined by her father)* Katerina. Ah luv yoo.

ALL. Congratulations!

(Scattered words as all but **ICHABOD**, **GUNPOWDER**, *and* **WOMEN** *repose and freeze.)*

ICHABOD. Congratulations. *(rises and begins to walk glumly to center)*

FIRST WOMAN. *(slowly)* Ichabod began his journey home.

He leapt upon Gunpowder and stumbled off down the road

Near the woods that creep along the churchyard and all the way down to the river.

*(***GUNPOWDER** *shadows* **ICHABOD**, *just up left of his position; he/she mimics* **ICHABOD***'s motions and moods. Reposed actors slowly begin to fold in sound effects – Gunpowder's walk, wind, owls, etc.)*

SECOND OLD WOMAN. His head hung low; his thoughts were far away.

He did not notice the deepening shadows of midnight as they gathered in the trees above him, nor Did he hear the rustle of leaves that seemed – almost! – to whisper his name.

(Increase effects, lights dim to 2 while a spotlight rises on **ICHABOD** *and* **GUNPOWDER**.*)*

THIRD OLD WOMAN. *(faster)* He had hardly reached the gates of the churchyard,

When he heard approaching fast behind,

The angry thunder of horse's hooves.

(Actor provides sound effect of horse by clapping hands and slapping knees one at a time.)

THIRD OLD WOMAN. *(cont.)* With lightening speed they crashed through the trees,

Coming straight toward him on the narrow road.

ICHABOD. The headless horseman!!! AHHH!!!

(GUNPOWDER mouths ICHABOD's scream.)

FOURTH WOMAN. *(Fast, urgent, beginning to speed with the mood but maintaining the meter, ICHABOD and GUNPOWDER perform the actions as outlined in the text.)*

And off he dashed, pushing Gunpowder towards the bridge at breakneck speed.

The frightened horse made hard for the river while the horseman followed, closer and louder.

FIRST WOMAN. As Ichabod reached the banks of the river,

Gunpowder started, and stuttered, and stalled,

and turned to bring Ichabod 'round face to face,

with a tall figure sitting astride a black horse.

As his quivering eyes climbed higher and higher,

Ichabod saw the tall figure framed against the black and midnight sky.

In the limitless stillness and silence that followed,

Ichabod raised his eyes to find that –

ICHABOD. *(whispered)* The horseman has no head.

SECOND WOMAN. And from the depths of the spirit a dark laughter came

(BROM provides laugh from repose, head down.)

That shook Ichabod down to each bone in his frame,

And made him cry out at the sound of his name –

ALL CAST. *(quick rise, out to audience, evil shouting)* Ichabod Ichabod Ichabod Crane.

(ICHABOD & GUNPOWDER ride even harder.)

FIRST WOMAN. But Ichabod was gone on a mad dash through night,

Determined to flee from the spirit he feared.

FIRST WOMAN & TWO. The black horseman reared and then joined in the chase,
Old Gunpowder ran like a young and strong stallion,

& THREE. He sped and he snorted and turned on the spot

& FOUR. But they could not escape from the dead soldier's laugh,
Or the sound of his hooves as they came fast behind,
Until, finally, Ichabod reached once again,
The gate of the churchyard and came to a halt.

ALL WOMEN. When he turned 'round to face the young Hessian,
He put back his shoulders and raised up his chin,
The soldier paused just for a moment before he brought up his hand slowly to show what he held.

*(**BROM**, head still low, eyes averted, slowly extends his arm to the audience and opens his empty hand.)*

As he raised the head higher,
His laugh grew much louder

*(**BROM** laughs again, devilishly.)*

And drove other sounds from the schoolmaster's ears,
Until finally the horseman released his dead burden,
And Ichabod's voice was made free in his scream.

*(**BROM** hurls invisible object. **ALL CAST** extend arms into the air. They scream – beat – and drop to the floor, except for the four **OLD WOMEN**, who return to the ever-so-slow, peaceful, rocking pace of the opening.)*

FIRST WOMAN. We haven't seen Ichabod since that dark evening.

SECOND WOMAN. His horse and he both disappeared in the night.

THIRD WOMAN. But late on some evenings just a minute to midnight –

FOURTH WOMAN. When the moon has not risen, and the wind is quite still –

FIRST WOMAN. You can hear if you walk near the woods by the churchyard –

SECOND WOMAN. A faint, thin voice whisper the schoolmaster's name –

THIRD WOMAN. *(whisper)* Ichabod –

FOURTH WOMAN. *(whisper)* Ichabod –

FIRST WOMAN. *(whisper)* Ichabod Crane.

(Momentary freeze. **WOMEN** *repose. Lights out.)*

OTHER TITLES AVAILABLE FROM BAKER'S PLAYS

GHOST RIDER

Steph DeFerie

10m, 11f / Thriller, Jr. High/High School / Simple set

The Williams family has just moved into their new house when they notice that things are a little strange; books fall off of shelves all by themselves, dolls go missing, and they all keep humming the same song, a song none of them had ever heard before. With the help of a physic and a historian, they discover that the house was a part of the underground railroad, and that a little runaway slave girl died in a secret hiding space in the wall. The action from 1855 takes place at the same time as the modern day, with the actors inhabiting the same space at times. Ultimately the modern family finds her poor little bones and decides that the right thing to do would be to carry them to Canada and bury them there, so that she can finally complete the journey she began over 150 years ago.

www.ingramcontent.com/pod-product-compliance
Lightning Source LLC
Chambersburg PA
CBHW071848290426
44109CB00017B/1970